Decisions!

Pragmatically Optimize your Decision-Making.

Howard Flomberg

Thank you to

Thirty Years of Students!

Forward

This little book has had a long journey. It started when I got to teach a course called Managerial Decision Theory at Metropolitan State College of Denver; I decided that I wanted to present both Quantitative and Qualitative decision theory. I started searching for a textbook and that book did not exist at that time. The only option I could find was to use two textbooks and hit the students for another couple hundred dollars in textbooks. I did not like this option. I decided to write my own. I had the entire summer to do it. I was a neophyte at writing a book and I did not realize that I was insane for trying to write a book in two months.

With the help of friends and colleagues, Management Decision Theory, Managing Pragmatically appeared. A second edition sprang to life in 2008. When I go back and read them, frankly, I am horrified. However, *I am now Published.* I retired from teaching in December 2009 and I wanted to write. I am taking the concepts in Management Decision Theory and convert the ideas into a book for the pragmatically oriented manager. Wish me luck!

Howard P. Flomberg, M.S.C.S.
Denver Colorado
October 12, 2010

Table of Contents

Introduction

Decision-making has been a black art for centuries. In the 20th Century, however, methods and procedures for decision-making have achieved some success, thanks to management science techniques. Making a decision is, by its very nature, a blend of qualitative and quantitative processes.

Qualitative analysis exists around scrutiny of observed or anticipated actions. This research technique demands an analyst who can maintain an objective view of the situation. However, when we discuss quantitative analysis, we think of numbers and quantities. The mind wanders to counting, statistics and probabilities, an uncomfortable place for many. This has been the standard domain for decision theory for decades.

Statisticians and the mathematically inclined consider qualitative analysis to be a stepchild. In contrast, a person who is involved in the decision making process often intuitively operates using qualitative analysis. Qualitative analysis makes use of that person's experience, expertise and professional opinions.

This study revolves around techniques that use both qualitative and quantitative approaches. Some of the tools that covered are: Bayes' Theorem, and the Delphi Method.

Bayes' Theorem evaluates the probability of an event happening with the assumption that past events can affect future events. Bayes' gives us a way of using history to predict the future. Mathematic Notation[1] is used to teach Bayes'. Most non-mathematicians are inexperienced or uncomfortable with this notation. Alternative methods include tree theory and table manipulation. In this text, we present Bayes' for the less-mathematically oriented reader.

---

[1] Mathematic Notation – See gobbelty-gook

The Delphi method is a formal way of gathering the appropriate people so that their management can make an informed decision. The technique comes from work done at the Rand Corporation in the 1950s. The technique was originally used to model the effects of nuclear war. It traces directly back to the operations research work done by the British during World War II. Military planners have used decision theory very successfully.

Decision-making depends on sound management principles. A well-run organization enables appropriate decisions. A poorly run organization frequently forces poor decisions. This book is essentially a toolbox that provides both qualitative and quantitative tools that will aide in decision-making. If the organization does not work, nothing else will.

I – Management Science

I define Management Science as: understanding the use of Mathematic, Computers and Science-based modeling tools to optimize decision-making. You will notice my use of the word "optimize." An optimal solution is one that exists in the real world. This may not be the best solution, however it is the most "workable" solution. One final note: The techniques and methods discussed herein can be superb tools. However, there are no replacements for the ultimate managerial tool, "Common Sense.[2]"

---

[2] com·mon sense (n)— Sound practical judgment derived from experience rather than study; Encarta® World English Dictionary ©1999 Microsoft Corporation. All rights reserved. Developed for Microsoft by Bloomsbury Publishing Plc

Problem Definition

You are driving along Interstate 25 north of the city of Cheyenne, Wyoming. Suddenly, you hear that annoying sound. It sounds like an airplane coming in for a landing. You get a sick feeling in the pit of your stomach. You have a flat tire. For those of you who have never been on Interstate 25 north of Cheyenne Wyoming, with the exception of a few antelope and scrub brush, there's no there, there. You pull over and check – yes, the tire is flat, and what do you do? What exactly is the problem that you have to solve? The obvious answer is:

"Hey stupid, I have a flat!"

Let us think about this situation. We will get back to our tire later.

Before we analyze the problem and make a decision, we must be aware that a problem exists and know what it is. In the tire example above, your problem seems to be that you are stuck on the side of the road with a flat tire, one hundred miles from anywhere. Is that the problem?

Frequently the apparent problem is not the real problem but is problematic, or a symptom. A symptom indicates a problem exists, however the occurrence of the symptom is not the problem. Fixing the symptom might feel good for a while, however the problem still exists. The successful manager must distinguish between the problem and the symptoms. Treating a gunshot wound with pain medication only addresses a symptom of the situation – it might alleviate the pain. It does not fix the wound. The arm still might fall off.

Another situation that the manager needs to deal with is the *bias*[3] built into the word, problem. The dictionary definition of the word *problem* is: "a question or puzzle that needs to be solved." I'll add to that definition. A problem exists only when a decision is needed[4].

---

[3] Be aware of your automatic bias about the word "bias"
[4] I must give credit to my Mentor, Joe D. Megeath, PhD, for that concept.

A problem is not necessarily a negative situation. A problem simply means that we must make a decision. If there is we do not have to make a decision, there is no problem, only a course of action. Problems can be either positive or negative. An opportunity can present itself that has choices. The selection of the choice can affect the return. The flat tire situation only indicates that there might be a problem. In the flat tire situation, we can assume that the problem is a negative one. Nevertheless, is the flat a problem? It is not. The flat is a state of nature. It exists. Deal with it.

"I have been selected to three colleges." Is that a problem? Actually, a problem does exist. What is a problem? Is there a problem? In this case, the problem is, "*Which College do I go to?*" When identifying a problem, you must also deal with bias: "We've always done it that way!" This bias may take the form of the timeworn statements like: "We have to live with that problem. It's not worth fixing."

A Real Life Problem (or is it a problem?)

Many years ago when I was a computer programmer, I was working on a customer's site, performing maintenance on the company's general ledger software. When I was looking for test data, my team leader, who was an employee of the company, pointed me to a file. As I was going through that file, I realized that I was actually in the real corporate ledger. Did they want me poking around in there? Then, when I started testing my software changes, I found that the books balanced to a $.23 difference. When I inquired, I was told that the "problem had existed for a while, no one wanted to spend the time to resolve it."

Was there a problem? Were there two problems? Perhaps, as my team lead thought there were no problems? Management obviously felt there were no problems. Is bias a problem? Does the fact that I was representing a trusted consulting firm enter into the situation? If you were the auditor, what would you say about this situation? I will come back to this also in a moment.

We can list some of the properties of problem definition. The list might contain:

- Who is the person who is making the decision (the Decision Maker)?
- At what level do we solve the problem? Can a team lead solve the problem or should he escalate it to the CEO ? Perhaps some level of authority between the two is adequate.
- What are you trying to do? What is the Big Picture? Do you want to maximize profit?
- Do you want to minimize cost?
- What are the constraints that influence the decision? They can be monetary, legal, geographic, ethical or even (?) governmental.
- Alternatives – What are the alternatives for you to consider? The alternatives are frequently mutually exclusive. Payoffs or Penalties – Each alternative should have payoffs or penalties. What are they?
- Review past situations. Can history present probabilities of success or failure?

Remember,

<p align="center">Doing nothing is always a valid alternative.</p>

In the Flat Tire situation, what are the possible actions? Should you change the tire? Call AAA? Wait for someone to pass by. Now, what is the problem? What if you are 75 years old and have a bad heart – does that affect the situation? Would the solution – or even the problem itself – it would be different it you were 23 years old and in perfect health? How do these differences affect the optimal solution?

In the "Real Life Problem" example, identify the problem(s).

In 1962, Rachel Carlson wrote the book Silent Spring. Many people consider this book to be the beginning of the ecology movement. You work for the Secretary of the Interior. He has read the book and has assigned you the responsibility of "Fixing the Problem." Identify the problem. Does that word _Malaria_ enter into your analysis? Given today's "Green Revolution" has the entire subject changed?

In 1911, a factory in New York City called, "The Triangle Shirtwaist Company," burned down. One hundred forty-six of the 500 people who worked there died. You work for the Mayor of New York. He called you into his office and told you to "Fix the Problem. Make sure that it never happens again" Identify the problem.

In 1965, Ralph Nader kicked off his career by publishing the book "Unsafe at any speed." This book killed the Chevrolet Corvair. You have an advance copy of the book. Your boss, the CEO of GM tells you to "Fix the Problem." Identify the problem.

You work for a major financial company. Your boss has been watching the giants' crumble and fall. He is nervous about spending time in "Club Fed[5]" for any oversight he might have missed. He has called you into his office and asked you to see if there is a problem, and if there is: "Fix the Problem." Is there a problem? Why or Why not? If there is a problem, identify it. What information do you need in order to establish what the problem is?

---

[5] Federal Prison

A series of complaints of sausages exploding when thawed out has been made to your Local Sausage Manufacturing Company. Using the steps listed below identify the problem.

1. Define the problem
2. Identify alternative solutions
3. Identify future returns, positive or negative
4. Select and implement a modeling technique
5. Decide

II - Quantitative (Numbers) Analysis

The Basics, Statistics and Probability

Do not run! You are NOT going to have to calculate means or standard deviations. You may have already labored through at least one course on Statistics. However, it is important to spend some time reviewing the ***application*** of statistics, simply to discuss what they mean and how to apply them in order to create a frame of reference for major topics.

For example, many years ago, upon graduating from college, I got a job as a Junior Programmer at an oil company. The first system I worked on, "Oil Flow Balance (OFB)" measured the efficiency of the refining process by measuring the amount of product as it flowed through each of the many vats. Management needed a report that extracted data from an existing file and produce a summary report on the amount of product in a series of vats. I was fresh out of college; therefore, I knew everything there was to know.

I wrote a report that analyzed the data in many directions – producing quantities to four decimal places. I was proud of the report and management loved it. Management had never had that level of accuracy before. Some weeks later, I found out the source of the numbers that I was calculating to four decimal places. A man would climb onto the vat with a long stick, stick it in the vat and read off the capacity. I was taking "It looks like 35,000 gallons" to a 4-decimal place number. Moreover, management bought it completely! The answer was accurate, or was it? How do we define accuracy? Is "Accurate" an accurate word?

Central Tendencies

Mean and Median

Mrs. Whitcomb[6], the often maligned and feared English teacher, wanted the "average" height of her students. She lines them up and measures them. Mrs. Whitcomb adds up their heights, divides that by the number of students in the class, 15. The average is 55 inches. In other words, the arithmetic mean is 55 inches. Next, Mrs. Whitcomb has them line up in size order and finds the student in the middle of the class – Karen and Norbert are both 57 inches. Coincidentally, they are standing in the middle of the line. The median height is 57 inches [note: being essentially lazy, I had Excel compute the mean and median]

Median -> 57

40, 44, 47, 48, 52, 53, 55, 57, 57, 58, 59, 60, 61, 61, 75

Mean -> 55

---

[6]In retrospect, Mrs. Whitcomb was the hardest teacher I ever had. However, I learned more from her than any other teacher I ever had. The emotional scars have healed rapidly yet the knowledge remains. Thank you Mrs. Whitcomb.

- Which "average" is more accurate, the mean of 55 inches or the median of 57?

- What do we mean by accurate? By the way, what can we say if the mean is equal to the median?

Standard Deviation

Ms. Whitcomb then wonders: how valid are these numbers? Is the mean truly representative of the class? She asks Marianne, who is taking an advanced placement class in statistics, to figure out how valid these numbers are. Marianne computes a standard deviation of 8.13 inches. She further explains: Assuming a normal distribution, the standard deviation is 8.13 inches. That tells me that 68% of the class is between 48.9 inches and 65.1 inches. Huh?

Mrs. Whitcomb, being confused at these numbers notices Edward, who is over 6 feet tall, clearly does not belong here. She discovers that Edward is in fact Howard's father. He is out of work so he is just hanging around the class. She banishes him to the lunchroom and has Marianne recalculate her numbers. With Edward removed, the mean is now 53.7 inches, the median is now 56 inches and the standard deviation is 6.7 inches. So we can deduce:

	With Edward	Without Edward
Mean	55	53.7
Median	57	56
Standard Deviation	8.13"	6.7"
+/- 1 Standard Dev. (68%)	48.9 through 65.1	47 through 60.4

Ok, now what does this mean?

Mean, median and standard deviation are ways of looking at a group of numbers and evaluating their "Central Tendencies." Mean and median tell us where the central point is. Mean tells us the arithmetic center; median tells us the physical center. If the mean and median are the same, (or reasonably close) we can say the distribution is, or approaches being normal, i.e. the famous Bell Shaped Curve. (Well, not quite, but we can live with that explanation for a while)

A normal distribution is identified by a set of data where:

Mean = Median

The distribution is symmetric[7] about the mean

---

[7] Symmetric – Both sides of the curve about the mean are identical

In addition, we identify a normal distribution by its mean and standard deviation. Standard deviation tells us how valid the mean is, or how well the data is clumped[8]. If you noticed, Edward's height clearly affects the class averages. When we kicked Edward out, the standard deviation went from 8.13 inches to 6.7 inches. The lower the standard deviation, the more accurate the mean is. The data is well "clumped," or gathered about the mean. We also know from our statistics class that a set of data that is normally distributed:

- The mean +/- 1 standard deviation covers approximately 68% of the population
- The mean +/- 2 standard deviations cover approximately 95% of the population
- The mean +/- 3 standard deviations cover almost all of the population
- Greater than +/- 3 standard deviations is an **Outlier** and is generally not considered statistically valid.

So now, without Edward we can say:
- ½ of the class is shorter than 57.7 inches tall

---

[8] By the way, I own the word Clumped. If you hear someone use it, let me know and I will split the return on the lawsuit. And yes, I'm joking

- ½ of the class is taller than 57.7 inches tall
- Approximately 9.52(10?) of the students are within one standard deviation of the mean.
- Approximately 13.3 (13?) of the students are within 2 standard deviations of the mean
- Approximately 13.6 (All?) of the students are within 3 standard deviations of the mean

Ok, granted, this a small sample: 14 people.

If you have a need to compute these numbers, Excel and many calculators[9] will do the job for you. The focus of the rest of this book will be in USING statistics, not calculating them. There is no need to show you how to compute the standard deviation.

---

[9] At our school we use the TI 83+

Calculating Percentages – Lets use this stuff.

You are making $1,000 per week working for Gosdork, Inc.; your boss comes to you and says that due to a problem with Balance of Trade he has to cut your salary by 50%

Pay Before Cut	$1,000
50% of Pay	$500
Pay after Cut	$500

The next month your boss says that he is restoring your 50% pay cut due to a new international agreement

Pay After Cut	$500
50% of pay	$250
"Restored" Pay	$750

28

What is the problem? On the other hand, is there a problem? From whose point of view is there a problem? Somehow, you are still down $250. Who's on first?

Remember these words: What is the base? The question that you should have been asking is "50% of what?" Need I go into detail? The technical term for this is playing fast and loose with numbers. But no one ever does that, do they?

Quantifiable vs. Qualifiable Variables

I love this example. The following article appeared on Network Television on January 24, 2005. MSNBC.COM listed it on their web site. The network thought it important enough run it again a year later on January 29, 2006. By sheer coincidence, it ran again in 2007. After three years, it *MUST* be true. In 2010 it is still running.

Jan. 24 called worst day of the year!

British psychologist calculates 'most depressing day' using a formula or model created by Dr. Cliff Arnal ... a U.K. psychologist:

$$([W + (D-d)] \, xTQ) / (M \, x \, NA)$$

Where:

- *(W) weather,*
- *(D) debt,*
- *(d) monthly salary,*
- *(T) time since Christmas, (Chanukah if Jewish?)*
- *(Q) time since failed quit attempt,*

- *(M) low motivational levels (NA) the need to take action.*

The article continued:

"I'm sure it's right," said Dr. Alan Cohen, spokesperson for the Royal College of General Practitioners, referring to Arnal's equation. ... However, "it is postulated that there are a number of different causes of depression," he said.

Discuss the reliability of this model (or lack thereof?)

You cannot reliably compute numbers that have no basis in reality. Then again – that is never done right? You have two children – a red-haired son and a blond daughter. What is their average hair color? Now a physicist might answer that question. But realistically, how many of us are physicists? You CANNOT make mathematically based statements, such as average (?) based on values that have no arithmetic relationship.

Percentages

Probability is probably the most intuitive of the management sciences. People flip coins, shoot craps and spin the roulette wheel, not understanding that they are dealing with probability. However, like many mathematics concepts, when you formalize and study it, probability loses much of its mystique. Simply put, probability is the way to deal with uncertainty.

- *"Mr. Jones, your 97- year-old grandfather has a 20 percent chance of surviving his operation."*
- *"If I buy a lottery ticket, I have just as much of a chance of winning 12 million dollars as anyone else does. Therefore, my odds of winning are 50-50[10]"*
- *"When you're in Vegas, put a dollar on number 17 for me."*

---

[10] I've heard this more than once.

Each of the above examples approaches an uncertain situation and uses probability to understand it. As a side note, on a standard Las Vegas roulette wheel, the odds of hitting a number are 38 to 1 (Numbers 1 to 36 plus 0 and 00). The house pays 35 to 1, hence, the house edge of 2.8% vs. 2.6%. Those two-tenths of one percent pay the rent!

Flipping a coin is the standard example of probability. The coin dictates the probability. Properly flipped, with an honest coin, the probability of the coin coming up heads is .5; every flip is independent, with the probability never changing. In other words, the coin does not have a memory. We refer to this as objective probability.

Probability can also be subjective. You are sitting in the airport waiting for your flight. You strike up a conversation with a pilot sitting next to you. He informs you that the probability of your aircraft exploding is one chance in 12 million. You relax and sit back comfortably. As you are sitting there, you see an airplane taxi down the runway, lift off and explode.

Now how confident are you in the 1 in 12 million odds? The probability has not changed, but your view of it has taken a severe hit. In this case, the probability as you perceive it, is highly subjective.

Some years ago, I was in an airplane returning from Florida. The weather was quite bad and we had to put in at Colorado Springs to refuel before continuing on to Denver. The flight had been bumpy and some people were quite uncomfortable. As the pilot restarted the engines, the wind switched and blew directly into the engine. The result was a rather dramatically large fireball coming from the engine. I spent enough time in the Air Force to realize that this was actually a normal situation; however, some people on the airplane panicked and demanded to leave and return to the terminal so that they could get off.

Looking at the situation objectively, we were in no danger. Subjectively, however, in some people's minds we were danger. Probability enables you to look at a situation and have some insight as to the preferable decision. At least give you the impression that you have insight. It took a man named Thomas Bayes[11] to actually put it all together and make it useable. Bayes looked at past events and their effect on future events. He did this by examining Conditional Probability and Joint Probability.

Bayes Rule (Conditional Probabilities)

We are investigating the probability of a person in a specific clinic having (or getting) cancer. Let us fill in the blanks. Suppose that we are looking at two situations:

- A person has cancer and/or
- A person is a smoker

---

[11] Reverend Thomas Bayes (c. 1702 - 1761) was a British mathematician and minister.

In our clinic, 10 percent of the people entering have cancer – By examination, we know that one half of our patients smoke or did smoke and we also know by checking with our patients that 80 percent of our cancer patients smoke or did at one time. If a person was a smoker, what is the probability of person having or getting cancer?

We compute the probability using the Bayes Rule:

$P(A|B) = ((P(B|A) P(A))/P(B)$ [12]

OK, I know I promised to keep it simple. Bear with me...

This can be interpreted as:

The probability of a person getting cancer GIVEN he is a smoker is equal to the probability of being a cancer patient who smokes, multiplied by the probability of having cancer. We divide this amount by the probability of being a smoker. Therefore – The probability of a smoker getting cancer – subject to the information that we have gathered – is 16%. I'll show you a much easier way of doing this

---

[12] Yuck – I agree!

This is an important and frequently ignored point. Bayesian probabilities can only apply if the specific case under examination is valid for the population it is applied it to. Given this situation, you cannot now take a group of high school athletes and tell them that 16 percent of the smokers in that group will probably get cancer (why?). However, you can say that any patient in this clinic who smokes or has smoked has a 16 percent probability of getting cancer. Does this mean that 16 percent WILL get cancer?

Bayes Theorem

You have made it this far. Take a deep breath, get a cup of coffee and hang on. It does get simpler. You run a plant that manufactures sausage. You purchase sausage casings from two plants, one in New Jersey and one in Connecticut. They both charge the same for their casings and transportation costs are similar. New Jersey produces 45 percent of your casings and Connecticut produces 55 percent. At the factory in South Bronx, we place all of the casings a common vat and then process them. After a rash of sausages exploding due to defective casings, the Quality Assurance (QA) manager determines that 5 percent of the New Jersey Casings are defective and 10 percent of the Connecticut casings are defective. The production manager, being a graduate of this school, decides to analyze the situation.

He decides that he needs to know the following:

- What is the probability of a casing being from New Jersey, given it is defective?
- What is the probability of a casing being from Connecticut, given it is defective?

There are three basic methods to present this problem. You can use the formula, use a tree diagram or use a table. I will present both the tabular approach and a tree diagram.

We should outlaw this formulaic method as cruel and unusual punishment.

Here's why: $PE(H) = [P(H)/P(E)] \, PH(E)$ Note: You may (should?) ignore this formula!

The Tabular approach

Events	Prior Probabilities	Conditional Probabilities	Joint Probabilities	Revised Probabilities
New Jersey	.45	.05	(.45)(.05) = .0225	.0225/.0775=.29
Connecticut	.55	.1	(.55)(.1) = .055	.055/.0775 = .71
Totals			.0775	1.00

Now we can reliability state the following:
- Approximately 8% (actually 7.75%) of our casings are defective
- Approximately 29% of the defective casings come from New Jersey

- Approximately 71% of the defective casings come from Connecticut

Now let's build a tree diagram:

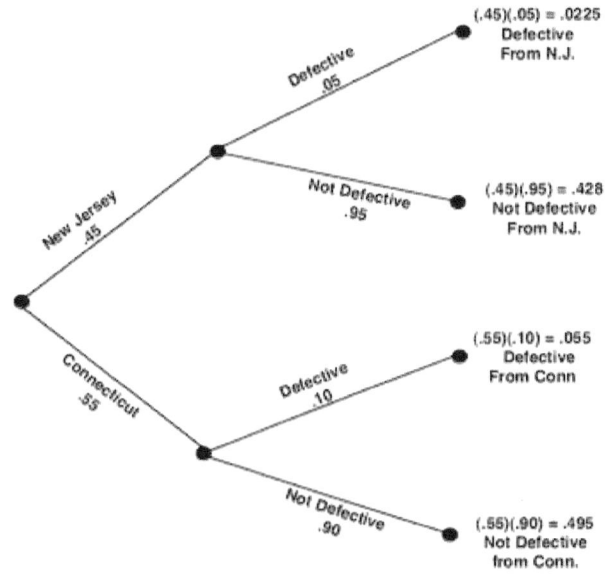

Can you follow this? IMHO[13] it is much easier to deal with than the other two approaches.

---

[13] IMHO = In My Humble Opinion

Riddle me this: Your neighbor makes fan belts. He also imports them from both New Jersey and Connecticut. Can he use these assumptions? Why or why not?

Next topic: Can we use quantitative analysis techniques on qualitative data? Here's an example: Suppose I survey the class and find out how many people have brown eyes, blue eyes or any other color. One might suppose that the distribution in a class of 30 people might be:

Eye Color	Count	Percent
Brown	21	70%
Blue	8	27%
Other	1	3%

If I choose a student at random, the probability that the student has brown eyes is 70 percent. The probability of the student having blue eyes is 27 percent. This is a valid use of the information. However, I have read that 99.5 percent of the residents of the nation of Inner Slobovia have brown eyes. Since 70 percent of the class has brown eyes,

I can therefore assume that 70 percent of the class is Inner Slobovian. What is wrong with this example? The Latin term is non sequitur, or, "it doesn't follow."

As foolish as this is, this type of reasoning is frequently observed and accepted as true.

Study Questions

1. You have a 1970 AMC Gremlin and the battery is going out. After a thorough search, you identify two batteries that interest you. Irving's Inimitable Batteries sells a model for your car that costs $250 and has a 2-year warranty. However, there is a 75 percent failure rate in year 3. Battery Bonanza has a model that is only $123.99 and comes with a 90-day warranty. The battery has a 23 percent failure rate for the first two years and a 90 percent failure rate in year 3. As you are a poorly paid college professor, you plan to keep your car for at least 10 more years.

- How do you decide which battery to choose?
- You can run a test that will tell you the anticipated lifespan for the battery.

The test has an 85 percent accuracy rate and costs $50. Would you pay for the test?

2. Of a population of 1,200 college students, 75 percent reside on campus. The remaining 25 percent live at home. Fourteen percent of the students who live on campus have contracted Beriberi, a rare tropical disease. Nine percent of those who live at home have contracted the disease. If a new drug to inoculate against the disease costs $17.25 per dose, how many doses should you purchase to protect those students who have not caught the disease?

3. A telemarketing company is analyzing its success ratio. They find that 23 percent of the calls that they make are answered successfully. Of these calls – 40 percent of the people called are college graduates, while 60 percent of those who answer did not complete college. Fifteen percent of the college graduates purchase the product, 43 percent of the non-college graduates purchase the product. :
Analyze the situation.
- How will this information affect your marketing program?
- They gathered this information during a sales program for a Life Insurance package.
- Can you use this data to predict sales for Car Insurance?

4.   I am looking at changing the vendors for hubs for my motorbike manufacturing company. I have selected two candidate vendors and asked them to submit 10 sample hubs selected at random for my examination. Here is a portion of a spreadsheet where I have run an analysis on the hubs. For each sample, I have listed the variance +/- from the standard measurement. I ran the analysis twice – First on the entire set of data. In the second run I trimmed the data by eliminating the highest and lowest numbers.

Which analysis do you give more credence to?

Which Vendor do you choose?

Hub Tests

Sample #	Vendor A	Vendor B
1	0.021	0.001
2	0.050	0.001
3	0.070	0.003
4	02075	0.004
5	0.100	0.005
6	0.124	0.023
7	0.125	0.070
8	0.126	0.200
9	0.300	0.230
10	0.300	0.856
Entire set of Data		
Mean	0.129	0.139
St. Dev	0.096	0.266
Trimmed Data		
Mean	0.121	0.067
St. Dev	0.078	0.094

Vendor B's sample 10 is in excess of three standard deviations from the mean. This is defined as an Outlier. An Outlier is a sample observation that, due to its value (+/- 3 standard deviations), is statistically insignificant. Traditionally, outliers are removed and the analysis redone. The trimmed test achieves that purpose. Does your analysis of the samples change because of this knowledge?

Risk Premium

Is it worth the risk to me? Let's play a game. I will flip a coin. If it lands with the head side up, I will give you $100. If the coin lands tail side up, I give you nothing. Oh, and it will cost you $50 to play. The probabilities here are intuitive. Fifty percent of the time you get a net $50 payoff. Fifty percent of the time you lose your $50 buy-in; would you play? What if your buy-in is $40? How about $25, would you play then? Risk Aversion is an important factor in decision-making.

Let us change the rules of this game a bit. I will give two options.

Option 1, I give you $50, or,

Option 2, we flip a coin and depending on the flip, you get either $100 or nothing.

Now there are three possible outcomes:

1.   You keep $50

2.   You have a 50% probability of getting $100

3.   You have a 50% probability of getting nothing

On the other hand, you might say – you have 100% probability of keeping $50. You have a 50% probability of making $100. You have a 50% probability of making nothing. Make your choice. How risk averse are you? Most people will take the sure thing.

However, let us decrease the amount of the Sure Thing. Do you go for the risk if the offer is $40? Do you go for the risk if the offer is $30? At what point do you choose to take the risk? The difference between that point and the original $50 is that amount is the risk premium. The Risk Premium is the reward for holding a risky investment rather than a risk-free one. If you choose to go for the risk at the $35 level, your risk premium is $15[14]

Insurance is a statement of Risk Premium. You insure yourself against loss depending on your willingness to take risk. Compare the person who takes a homeowner's policy with a $1000 deductible against a person who chooses to pay the additional amount of $15 per year over the life of the policy for a $200 deductible policy.

---

14   McMillin, Games, Strategies & Managers.

III - Regression

In your Mathematics 311 class, you start wondering whether the amount of studying really has an effect on the final grade. You notice that the entire class consists of people with approximately the same educational background and level of intelligence. You ask them to track the number of hours that they spend studying and their final grade. You get this result:

Name	Hours	Grade
Aaron	60	85
Betty	48	85
Charlie	52	74
Donna	47	71
Edward	73	99
Frankie	55	72
Georgette	53	85
Howard	23	70
Joe	58	60
Karen	57	87
Louis	72	90

Marianne	44	52
Norbert	57	87
Otto	61	95
Peter	61	87

You ask the class genius, Edward to do some research and he finds you a tool called Linear Regression. Linear regression looks at two sets of numbers and determines whether there is a relationship between them, i.e., can one set be used to predict the other. Well, all that being said, Edward finds an Excel tool and crunches the numbers. He comes back and tells you:

The R-Squared is .36.

WOW, now you know! "Get back here Ed. What does that mean?" Simply put – Linear regression produces a formula by which you can use one variable to predict another. For this specific table, the regression formula is:

Grade = 44.0 + 0.656 Hours, with an R-Sq of .36 OR - if you take the number of hours that a person studied and multiplied that number by .656, then added 44 to it, you would get an approximation of the grade that they would receive.

How good an approximation is it? The "coefficient of determination", or R-Squared (R-Sq), is the number that tells us how good the fit is. The higher that the R-Sq is the better the fit is. If the R-Sq is a negative number, we have a negative correlation, .36 is a weak correlation. For example, .99 would be a superb correlation.

Regression analysis is a powerful tool for forecasting. However, like any tool, you cannot blindly use it. It still requires management thought for the tool to be effective. The job of a manager is to make decisions; we use these quantitative tools to provide information for decision-making. They are not for blindly making decisions.

Excel can do the messy calculations.

Case Study: Richman Courier Service

1. Which car should we buy?

Mr. Max Richman runs a courier service. He primarily delivers legal forms. At times, however, he has to provide a chauffeur for in-city transportation in the downtown section of a medium sized American city. He has a fleet of approximately 30 vehicles. Ever year he trades in one-third of his fleet. Therefore, you can assume that he currently has 10 2005s, 10 2004s and 10 2003s. Mr. Richman has inherited his business from his father-in-law and has been hesitant to change anything.

He has a mix of mid-size 4-door sedans with 6 cylinder automatic power trains. He always buys a base trim. His fleet is essentially a 50-50 mix of Chevrolet Malibu and Ford Taurus automobiles.

Mr. Richman anticipates an increase in business and anticipates trading in his 10 oldest cars and purchasing 15 new ones. His father-in-law has departed[15], he is anxious to increase his profitability. Some of the questions he has are:

---

[15] He's dead, Jim

- What effect will the prevailing interest have on his decision?
- As the cost of gasoline increases does he have to make any modifications to his fleet?
- Should he look at alternative fuel sources?
- Is his current 3-year cycle effective?
- Are there any alternatives to using cars?

Using the six-step process that follows, analyze the available information and provide a recommendation for your client.

1) The Decision Maker – Who is the person who is making the decision? At what level does the problem have to be solved? Can a team lead solve the problem or do we need to escalate it to the CEO? Perhaps some level of authority between the two is adequate; why or why not?

2) The Goal –– What is the problem! What are you trying to do? What is the Big Picture? Do you want to maximize profit? Do you want to minimize cost? Are these two options always different?

3) Constraints – What are the constraints that influence the decision? They can be monetary, legal, geographical, ethical or even governmental.

4) Alternatives– What are the alternatives for you to consider. The alternatives are frequently mutually exclusive. Doing nothing is usually a valid alternative.

5) Payoffs or Penalties–– Each alternative should have payoffs or penalties. What are they?

6) Probabilities– review past situations. Can history present probabilities of success or failure?

Your intern has provided the following information: Illustration 1: Vehicle Comparison Chevrolet Malibu vs. Ford Taurus

In addition, Mr. Richman has paid for a study of business conditions in his region and has the following information in addition to the Prime Rate statistics.

There is a 42% probability that the next two years will present a steady growth rate of 15% per year

There is a 38% probability that the next two years will be stagnant

There is a 20% probability that the next two years will present a decline in the area with a 15% decline per year

Mr. Richman estimates that he can invest $300,000 in his facility.

What other information can you deduce?

What can you NOT deduce?

One last question: If the Environmental lobby loses a key decision in Congress, the ANWR oil reserves will be developed. This will cut oil prices by approximately 20 percent. You estimate that there is a 55 percent chance of this happening. Review all of your decisions and discuss the possible effect that this will have.

IV - Fuzzy Logic and the power of Iteration

I am not sure where this topic goes, or even if it belongs in this discussion. I will put it here – right between Quantitative and Qualitative, a fuzzy warm place, so it can at least feel like it belongs.

You step into a shower. The water is too hot. You turn the temperature knob to the right. You wait a while. The water is too cold. You turn the knob to the left a bit. Now the water is too hot again, but not as hot as before. You turn it to the right again, then left and then right. Eventually the water is just right. This "goldilocks and the three bears" approach to problem solving is Fuzzy Logic.

Fuzzy logic is a trial-and-error approach to problem solving. Perhaps this is a bit simplistic, but it is accurate. We apply Fuzzy Logic to control applications especially in manufacturing environments. Fuzzy Logic is a Rule-based approach[16]. Once you have defined the environment, you establish the rules. In a temperature control situation, two rules might be:

1.   If the temperature exceeds a target temperature, turn on the fan.

2.   If the temperature falls below a different target temperature, turn off the fan.

16 http://www.aptronix.com/fide/whyfuzzy.htm

By modifying the two target temperatures, we can regulate the effectiveness of the algorithm. Fuzzy Logic reduces the design development cycle. During the development, you can tune the process by simply modifying the rule set. Fuzzy Logic simplifies design complexity. A rule set is designed in simple English-like sentences. Fuzzy Logic improves time-to-market. A simpler product is easier to get off the production line and into the store. The simpler product is less problematic and easier to debug and fix. The power of fuzzy logic is iteration. As we will see, iteration is a tool that we use heavily in modeling.

V - Incompatibility Thesis AKA Bunk!

Those of us raised in the mathematic disciplines view qualitative techniques as somewhat irrelevant. While we do the "real" analysis in a mathematically based environment, we do qualitative analysis in the social and behavioral sciences. Any mathematician worth his salt "knows" that these are not real sciences. There is a thesis called the "Incompatibility Thesis" [17] which states that there is a profound difference between qualitative and quantitative techniques. Social Scientists long believed that they do not bind research by quantifiable observations. This school or thought felt that social science inquiry was value-free, that time- and context-free generalizations were possible, and that real causes to social scientific outcomes could be determined reliably.

---

[17] Howe, K.R. (1988) Educational Researcher

In fact, there exists a continuum with purists and pragmatists lying at opposite ends. The standard belief is that one school best analyzes some subjects. The other school best analyzes other subjects. The focus in these arguments is over the differences between them. Qualitative researchers discuss the superiority of in-depth research into the relationships between the causing agent and its results. Arguments raised against mixed-method research include the concept that researchers trained in one discipline cannot do justice to another.

Think of two carpenters discussing the relative merits of a Phillips-head screwdriver versus a flat-head screwdriver. They are both valid and useful tools. However, the type of screw in hand tends to direct the choice of product.

While we group tools, and many things, into the two categories, they tend to have a tendency to involve, and perhaps define, each other. In statistics, we have both descriptive and inferential statistics. Descriptive statistics rely upon observation and measurement. These statistics describe the state of the data. Inferential statistics take the descriptive statistics and use them to make inferences or assumptions about the data. Perhaps when you make assumptions, you are delving into the qualitative arena? On the other hand, the Social Sciences are replete with statistical analysis. The principle complaint against this practice is the question as to whether they are quantifying Qualifiable variables. For instance: In an earlier chapter, I presented a chart to represent the distribution of eye color in a group of 30 people.

As I presented the material earlier, the entire concept of "Average eye color" is obtuse. However, we can us this chart to predict the probability of a member of the group's eye color. We are successfully using a quantitative tool in a qualitative environment. Simply stated, the pragmatist says accurately

"Use the tool that makes the most sense"

VI - Ethical Pragmatism

Pragmatism

A definition of pragmatism is:

prag·ma·tism [18]. —

1. Philosophy. A movement consisting of varying but associated theories, originally developed by Charles S. Peirce[19] and William James and distinguished by the doctrine that the meaning of an idea or a proposition lies in its observable practical consequences.

2. A practical, matter-of-fact way of approaching or assessing situations or of solving problems.

In other words, doing what works. However forgive me for being trite, but do the ends justify the means?

---

[18] http://www.answers.com/pragmarism
[19] Nope, that's not a typo.

Ethics

Ethics is a general term for the study of morality. Ethical behavior is that which is "good" or "right." Let us discuss ethics from two divergent points of view.

Objectivism - Ayn Rand

Rand founded her philosophy of Objectivism on three axioms:

1) Reality is real

2) Everything has a specific nature

3) People possess a consciousness, an awareness, of reality

In contrast to the traditional altruistic belief that morality should benefit others, Objectivism argues that the beneficiary of one's moral code should be oneself. [20] Objectivists say that if everyone acted in a similar way society would function in a better manner.

---

[20] http://www.psychologicalscience.org/observer/getArticle.cfm?id=1820

Judeo-Christian view

We base morality is upon the God's law, i.e. the Bible. We have free will to decide whether to follow good or evil. God wants man to be ethical (Not evil). While objectivism regards reason as an absolute, The Judeo-Christian view holds that we base all knowledge on the evidence of the senses.

Objectivism holds that we establish all beliefs, conclusions and convictions by logical methods of inquiry. These are tested by logical methods of inquiry and logical methods of verification. In short, it holds that the scientific approach applies to all areas of knowledge.

> "... One does not live for the sake of being moral; one acts morally in order to make the most out of his life.[21]"

---

[21] David Kelley34

Therefore, with all this in mind, I define Ethical Pragmatism as: Doing "what works best" while mindful of the obligation one has to society. What is our obligation to society? American Ambassador William JU. Hudson said the following in a speech in Tunis:

> "Pragmatism is one of the distinctive aspects of the American way of doing business... American business leaders dislike theory. They are constantly looking for things that work – an organizational technique, a marketing strategy, or a financial tool – whatever it is, they are seeking results, and are not much interested in the theory that may underlie the approach they take. The great inventor Thomas Edison is still admired in the U.S. for perfecting the light bulb. This is not because of the elegant theories he proposed that led to a light bulb. It is because he kept stubbornly trying different solutions – by some counts over 2,000 – until he found the one that worked."

VII - Qualitative Analysis

Up to this point, we have been looking at Quantitative models. We have used statistics and probabilities to model the environment to provide information so that a manager can make a decision. Quantitative analysis is another way to gather and analyze information.

In his book "blink," Malcolm Gladwell discusses the concept of Adaptive Unconscious. Gladwell tells us this part of the mind makes quick decisions. We fertilize our mind by all of our years learning the industry in which we function[22]. Numbers and statistics can aid this decision-making process but it cannot replace it. Not all of the tools in the world can replace your expertise. Keep this concept in the back of our minds as we proceed. Let us look at some of the qualitative-based modeling techniques that have become prominent.

---

[22] If, like me, you're an NCIS fan, Special Agent Gibb's famous "Gut Instinct" is a superb example of this.

The JAD

Let me briefly fall back into my own experience. Developing a computerized information system is an engineering process. Unfortunately, the software engineering discipline is only a few decades old while formal engineering goes back to the builders of the pyramids. We had to learn the processes the hard way. Eventually we came up with a standardized 5-step system:

1. Requirements
2. Analysis or Business Design
3. Design or Technical Design
4. Construction Implementation
5. Acceptance

Requirements, analysis and design involve writing documents that frequently cross department boundaries. Many disciplines may be involved. All must sign off or the project is seriously impacted. The meetings can be endless and the process of finalizing the documents can become Herculean. In the late 1970s, IBM developed the concept of the Joint Application Design (JAD) Session. The concept is simple. You gather all the important people in a room **off-site**. Collect their cell phones, feed them and keep them there until the analysis or design document is complete. It sounds brutal, but it works. The participants generally include:

- Facilitator – a person trained in the JAD methodology that facilitates the discussion and enforces the rules.

- Technical Writer – A person who can transcribe the results in a timely manner.

- End Users – the people who have an actual piece of the pie. The people who will use the product that will eventually be produced.

- Developers – the technicians who will be building the product

- SME's – Subject Matter Experts.

The Facilitator does not have to be technically immersed in the topic; however, the facilitator must be able to control the JAD Session and keep it on track. A trained and/or experienced facilitator is crucial. The presence of a tech writer also makes a major difference. If the participants can see the written word immediately there is a minimum of, "That wasn't what I said." If a CASE[23] Tool is used, the tech writer is especially effective.

The strength of a JAD session is obvious; weeks of work can be compressed into days. A JAD session is effective in an environment where there is a defined development methodology. If there is no existing framework to apply the JAD against, the session degrades into "just another meeting."

---

[23] CASE – Computer Aided Software Engineering – A computer based tool that can be used to massively simplify the actual design and implementation of a computer system.

A (the?) major problem with any committee-based tool is that there is a short-lived group memory. After a day or so, the participants will no longer agree with specificity those ideas that they agreed upon during the meeting. The addition of items: A technical writer and a graphics-based CASE tool allow the group to come to agreement. This agreement depends on upon deliverable, fact-based documents. The result of this activity can be termed a Prototype

Ok, you are now asking: does all of this apply to my marketing problem? Bear with me for a while.

Prototyping

Brainstorming

A brainstorming session can be very successful, if we follow the rules. The rules are easy:

- Everyone takes turns proposing ideas.
- No ideas are ruled out for ANY reason.
- All of the ideas are recorded.

Once the brainstorming completes, we record the ideas and another smaller committee reviews them and moves forward. As we will see, the brainstorming session becomes the bedrock of many qualitative decision techniques. You come out of a brainstorming session with a set of solutions or actions. The set of rules might be ponderous, however, it belongs to the entire committee. The next step is obvious: a small team reviews all of the suggestions, prioritizes them and evaluates them.

The Straw Man

Another very powerful tool is a Straw Man. A committee is a poor way to develop a document. Committees tend to be populated by people waiting for "someone else" to get started. Therefore, to get the inertia going, have someone build a document as a starting point before the meeting. At the meeting, present this "Straw Man" document and let the group modify it. The person writing the document must be aware that his document is not going to survive in the form that it started.

Brainstorming and the Straw Man approach have one weakness in common. They do not remove the ego from the situation. People tend to take ownership of documents and ideas. If you criticize either one, you are criticizing the individual. Brainstorming opens to floor to all ideas equally. A Straw Man has the presupposition that the document will be a starting point. If a manager of, for that matter, a strong-willed person is in the session the meeting will become that person's meeting. Another word for that is "Ego".

The Jury of Executive Opinion

The Jury of Executive Opinion has become the catch phrase for a number of modeling techniques. The definition of this technique is that it is: "...A method of forecasting using a composite forecast prepared by a number of individual experts. The experts form their own opinions initially from the data given, and revise their opinions according to the others' opinions. Finally, the individuals' final opinions are combined[24]"

---

[24] http://www.bankofbaku.com/utilities/glossary/jj.htm

In other words:

- A group of "Executives" are gathered into the jury and presented with a problem (or most likely a problematic situation).

- Members of the jury form their own opinion as to the solution to the problem.

- The Jury reviews all of the solutions and develops a consensus.

- With a group of executives, a consensus may be impossible. Tying up a group of executives can be a very expensive affair.

- Scheduling becomes a nightmare – communication is nearly impossible.

While traditionally used as a forecasting tool, the jury works on many forms of decision analysis. A JAD session is a form of this process. The thrust of this procedure is using multiple people's expertise to solve a specific problem. The disadvantages are many in this raw form. A JAD session works around this by placing the focus in a trained facilitator.

The Delphi Method

In the early 1950s, the RAND Corporation did a study for the United States Air Force. The Air Force aimed the study at forecasting future Department of Defense technology needs in the face of a nuclear attack by the Soviet Union. This study, "Project Delphi," laid the groundwork for effectively using teams of experts for decision-making. The Delphi Method is a method of obtaining and refining group judgments. The Delphi Method contains three features:

1.   Anonymous response

2.   Iteration and controlled feedback

3.   Statistical analysis of the response

These procedures can remove the "ego" problems often associated with strong-minded individuals. While the Delphi Method is usually applied to forecasting, the model lends itself to any complex decision making situation. It has been used in industry with increasing frequency. In 1969 a RAND study was conducted comparing the Delphi Method to face-to-face interaction:

"The results indicated that, more often than not, face-to face discussion tended to make the group estimates less accurate, whereas, more often than not the anonymous controlled feedback feature made the group estimates more accurate.[25]"

A JAD session involves a group of users and technology-based people looking at resolving a set of specifications. The Delphi Method is aimed at broader set of decision makers. Traditionally, group consensus is reached through face-to-face meetings. These meetings tend to have certain obstacles:

• Certain dominant individuals can sway the group simply through their presence.

• A chief executive or simply a person who talks a lot can easily sway the group.

• Keeping a group on track is frequently a major problem. People bring their own interests into a meeting. You can depend on the meeting veering away from problem solving easily.

---

[25] Dalkey, Norman C. The Delphi Method: An Experimental study of Group Opinion, Santa Monica CA: The RAND Corporation, 1969, page vi.

- Peer pressure will discourage an individual from disagreeing with a popular opinion.

- Arranging a meeting imposes scheduling restriction. Finding a time and place that can suit multiple people is frequently extremely hard.

- The cost of getting people in that room can be high. Their time is dedicated to the purpose of the meeting, exclusively.

- Meetings must be documented to be effective. This frequently does not happen.

While the Delphi method is not a panacea, it is a good workable remedy for many of these problems. Delphi provides the benefits of pooling and exchanging opinions amongst participants in the consensus group so that they can each learn from each other without the inherent problems of face-to-face meetings.

The Delphi Method optimally uses both the qualitative and quantitative knowledge of a group of selected experts. It can be used to identify concepts that are relative to long range planning. It attempts to solidify complexities to single statements that can be analyzed.

"The ... Delphi method's unique strength is that it incorporates education and consensus building into the multistage process of data collection, thus enabling description of agreement about specific ... options among key players.[26]"

The Delphi method will not predict the future; it will aid in being prepared for it. As with any tool of this type, there are no firm laws governing the implementation of the tool. The steps that I provide are a suggestion drawn from experience and expertise of the literature of the field.

---

[26] Rayens, Hahn / Consensus Via Policy Delphi Method

Step 1: Selecting the panel of Experts

Since a Delphi is conducted by correspondence as opposed to gathering people in a single room, there are fewer limitations on the size of the panel. Putting more than seven or eight people in a room for a committee meeting seems to be exceeding the limit of effectiveness. Size is not nearly as much of a hindrance in a Delphi. A large group of experts lends credibility to both statistical analysis as well as the results. The person, or office, sending out the invitation will have a definite influence on the number of people who choose to respond. A CEO, for instance, will generate more response than a supervisor.

You want a blend of backgrounds. If you only contact accountants, or restrict invitations to marketing types, you will slant the results of the Delphi. Subject Matter Experts (SME's) come at all levels and hide in the most innocuous places. Some time might be spent informally discussing the Delphi with some "Old Hands" to root out the SME's

You do not want to use invitations as a status symbol. Remind those participating that their responses will be handled anonymously. How many? Select a number somewhere between 10 and 1000. This ambiguity is intended. The topic and environment will be the deciding factor.

Step 2: Questionnaire #1

The first questionnaire is, by intent, general. The purpose of this questionnaire is to establish the direction of the Delphi. For example[27], in one situation in a medical clinic, a Delphi was constructed to answer the following question:

"What action could be taken to provide faster response to patient inquiries between visits?"

Questionnaire #1 should be constructed as follows:

---

[27] http://instruction.bus.wisc.edu/readings/delphi.htm

The purpose of this questionnaire is to elicit your ideas regarding the following issue:

What action could be taken to provide faster response to patient inquiries between visits?

Please engage in individual brainstorming so as to generate as many ideas as possible for dealing with this issue. Please list each idea in a brief, concise manner. Your ideas do not need to be fully developed. If fact, it is preferable to have each idea expressed in one brief sentence or phrase. Your ideas will be anonymously included in the next questionnaire.

Idea # 1:

Idea # 2:

Idea # 3:

Idea # 4:

Idea # 5:

Step 3 Questionnaires #2 through n

Once the questionnaires are returned, they are collated. Identify which suggestions are most frequently made, combine them if possible. You might have to reword the results, however, be careful not to change the meaning. Publish the list, asking the respondents to evaluate each suggestion according to the following criteria:

1) Reliability —

a) Very Reliable

b) Reliable

c) Unreliable

d) Very Unreliable

2) Desirability

a) Very Desirable

b) Desirable

c) Undesirable

d) Very Undesirable

3) Feasibility

a) Very Feasible

b) Feasible

c) Unfeasible

d) Very Unfeasible

Publish and distribute the list to your panel of experts with the ideas from the first questionnaire. When you publish the list, ensure that all ideas are presented with no attribution or any indication as to the popularity of the idea. When the next set of questionnaires are returned, you have a list of ideas that can be evaluated quantifiably. Evaluate the list and the results and compute the ideas that score the highest. Eliminate the ideas that perform the poorest and reformat the second questionnaire. If you assign a point value in the range of 4 (Very Positive) through 1 (Very Negative), a statistical analysis of the results can be taken. Then eliminate the poorest responses and the step is repeated. One caution: have an even number of options for the panel to from which to select. If there is an odd number – you usually will find a predominant number have chosen the middles response. An even number forces some thought. Review this questionnaire when it is returned and repeat the process

After two or three iterations, you should have the list down to a small number of workable solutions.

Step 4 Evaluations

Now that you have a smaller number of workable solutions, keep in mind: this has been a Consensus Building exercise. The remaining solutions are those wherein there is a consensus of the respondents as to a workable solution. Which of them is best? You might:

- Redo the Delphi with a smaller group of experts starting with the results that have been gathered.
- Bring in a select group of SME's and ask them to come up with the final solution
- Make a decision.

In the last chapter of his book "Blink," Gladwell discusses an extremely talented female trombonist who tried out for a prominent European orchestra. The European tradition was that a trombone was a "man's instrument." The idea of a woman being able to play this horn was unthinkable. She was turned down in audition after audition, however, in a blind audition where the player was behind a curtain, the woman repeatedly demonstrated her abilities and succeeded.

The Delphi is that curtain. The process of evaluating the input is handled "behind a curtain" so that the individual who is submitting the information cannot influence the value of the information.

And in Conclusion

The Theory of Constraints[28]

The Theory of Constraints is a management philosophy developed by Eliyahu M. Goldratt. TOC is a systems approach based on the assumption that every company, or for that matter, system, has at least one process that causes a bottleneck, reducing the company's ability to meet its goals. TOC allows maximizing profit by assuring that the factor that limits production (The Constraint) is used most efficiently. Both eastern and western forms of self-defense or Martial Arts have one thing in common –balance. However, in many western forms of self-defense such as boxing, the combatants use their own strength to destroy their opponent. In many Eastern forms of self-defense, the combatants seek to use their opponent's strength against them.

---

[28] Goldratt, The Goal

The Essence of TOC

"Find the essence of each situation, like a logger clearing a logjam. The pro climbs a tall tree and locates the key log, and blows it, and lets the stream do the rest. An amateur would start at the edge of the jam and move all the logs, eventually moving the key log. Both approaches work, but the essence concept saves time and effort.

Almost all problems have a key log if we learn to find it."

—Fred Smith, Information Systems theoretician and programmer

Implementing TOC

The original Goldratt "process of ongoing improvement" is:

1. Identify the system's constraint(s)

2. Decide how to exploit the constraint(s)

3. Subordinate everything else to the above decision

4. Elevate the constraint

5. If, in any of the above steps, the constraint has been broken, go back to Step 1

Obviously, this becomes iterative. As we identify and control a constraint, another constraint might become critical. If you do this more than three times, chances are, there is a deeper problem. Therefore, what do we change? Have we been attacking symptoms or problems?

• Locate the Constraint – the bottleneck. Define the Problem.

• As we control the constraint, we control the process.

• We must be aware of erroneous perceptions, assumptions and paradigms.

What do we change to?

• Focus on global performance, rather than local performance

If "What to change" are the existing but erroneous perceptions, paradigms, and assumptions, then to what to change to must start with their replacement.

Applying TOC

TOC has a strong relationship to classical Critical Path Method (CPM). CPM allows us to examine all possible relationships within the process and identify the path that takes the most resource. This path is the critical path. TOC similarly identifies the system constraint that is crucial – the "weakest link." This constraint is the place on which to concentrate our efforts. Once these constraints are managed, other constraints must be observed else they become critical. As we address a constraint, we eventually get it under control. At that point, we locate the next constraint that affects the system and repeat the analysis and improvement process.

TOC differs from classical cost accounting in that the effort places emphasis on variable expenses rather than fixed expenses. Fixed expenses are not adjustable; the variable expenses can be directly related to production, or the lack thereof.

A fundamental principle of this process is illustrated by the example of liquid pouring out of a bottle. Intuitively we realize that the width of the bottle opening constrains the amount of liquid pouring out. However, if we do some classical problem analysis we realize that the one constraint is the air coming into the bottle to replace the liquid. Every freshman high school science course addresses this one. By shaking the bottle in a circular manner, we get a mini-whirlpool that allows air to enter more rapidly and allows the liquid to exit more rapidly as well.

While the first analysis indicated the major constraint was the size of the opening, with further analysis we realized that the primary constraint (the actual problem, perhaps?) was getting air into the bottle. The limiting factors which affect the ability of a factory to produce a product over a period of time is similar to getting the water out of the bottle.

While this is a gross simplification, there is a running commonality through the topic of Decision Theory on identifying and addressing the problem, not the symptoms.

Thin Slicing

In my Undergrad days, I took a programming course called Advanced Fortran. This obviously was a course covering the finer points of the programming language FORTRAN. FORTRAN, An acronym for Formula Translation, was the one of the first high-level computer languages and a direct predecessor of BASIC.

One of the principle structures in FORTRAN is a Do Loop. A Do Loop is a set of commands that allow the program to iteratively repeat a series of instructions until some condition is complete. An example might be:

```
num = 0
do 10 i = 1, 10
   num = i
   write(*,*) "num =", num
10 continue
```

This chunk of code will print the numbers from one to ten. Do not worry if this seems like a Serbo-Croatian love-poem. I just wanted to make a point. FORTRAN also has a structure called an "Implied Do Loop". This structure provides some additional functionality:

1) The use of an Implied Do Loop allows you to combine multiple, complex statements into one incredibly long and cumbersome statement.

2) The use of an Implied Do Loop provides job security. It is nearly impossible to decipher another's code, especially while solving a production problem at 2:00 in the morning.

I was taking a test in class one day. The test involved writing a program that would print checkerboard pattern on the printer. This is a common test question for this subject. It forces the student to think using Loops. While I was digging through the code that I was writing, I realized that I could write the entire program with one three-line long implied do-loop. I have no idea how it really worked; I just knew that it would. I turned in my test with this statement. About a week later, I had my test returned with full credit. Written on it was this comment:

Howard,

If you ever do this to me again, I will kill you

- Professor Brown

Apparently, Professor Brown had to travel into the computer lab (This was before PCs and Online access) and type in the code that I had written in order to test it. The code worked. I do not know how or why, but I knew it would work.

How often have you met someone and instantly formed a dislike or, for that matter, an instant like for that person? You do not know why, but you do. Our minds constantly gather information and provide it to us. Malcolm Gladwell describes this rapid cognition in his book Blink. He calls this process Thin Slicing. Thin slicing is the act of relegating the decision-making process to, what Gladwell calls, the adaptive unconscious by focusing on a small set of key variables, as opposed to consciously considering the situation as a whole over as much longer period of time.

Thin slicing is also done consciously. The main characteristic of thin slicing is that only a few key factors are considered in the decision process. Even if more information is available, it is classified as irrelevant and discarded. The success of thin slicing in several situations is described in Blink. The idea of thin slicing challenges the commonly held belief that "more information is better" when making good decisions.

I hope that you got to the point where you have to make key decisions the hard way. You worked your way up the proverbial ladder, rung by rung[29]. On your way to management, you learned many lessons. You absorbed the "feel" of the job. A large amount of knowledge is with you, intuitively, whenever you are at work. Gladwell defines this adaptive unconscious[30] as the part of our brain that leaps to conclusions. He describes this adaptive unconscious as a "kind of giant computer that quickly and quietly processes a lot of the data we need in order to keep functioning as human beings." Gladwell cites the example of a person walking across a street. When he sees a truck bearing down upon him, he does not have time to ponder all of the options available. If he is to survive, he jumps out of the way. This is the essence of thin slicing.

---

[29] I love a good cliché
[30] *Blink*, pg. 11

As a manager, you are asked to evaluate a series of options to solve a particular problem. You review the options critically and decide which option is optimal for the solution. You instinctively know that the optimal solution is wrong. You cannot explain it, however your gut tells you that to follow the numbers is wrong. What do you do? Repeatedly, when I did not follow my gut instinct I made the wrong decision."

An article in Federal Computer Weekly, "Exploring intuitive decision-making[31]" discusses the topic, referring to it as Intuitive Decision Making:

---

[31] http://www.fcw.com/article78285

"...Instead of trying to deliver a perfect picture of the battlefield, we need to shift from that because the battlefield is chaotic and commanders are trained early on in their careers to make decisions based on their experience, intelligence and intuition," McAbee told Federal Computer Weekly... "One shoe doesn't fit all," McAbee said. "We need to tailor that stimulus. I think it will be incremental and we may never [fully] develop the system, but we need to start down that road and start developing the system in some areas to assist commanders in intuitive decision making."

Thin Slicing, Intuitive Decision Making and Gut Instinct[32]; they are all terms that relate quite closely. One of the dangers in decision-making is, as discussed above, excessive information. Thin slicing is an alternative – weigh your gut against the available options.

---

[32] If you're a fan of the TV show "NCIS" as I am, the character Gibbs is constantly referring to "Gut Instinct" and his gut is almost always right. Perhaps he's thin slicing?

Strategic Petroleum Reserves

The U.S. Strategic Petroleum Reserve is the largest stockpile of government-owned emergency crude oil in the world. Established in the aftermath of the 1973-74 oil embargo, the SPR provides the President with a powerful response option should a disruption in commercial oil supplies threaten the U.S. economy. It also allows the United States to meet part of its International Energy Agency obligation to maintain emergency oil stocks, and it provides a national defense fuel reserve. [33] You have been appointed to a committee of businessmen and politicians. The committee's purpose is to control the use of these reserves. You are to develop a set of guidelines controlling:

      1.   The circumstances that would entail the distribution of oil

      2.   The means of distribution

      3.   The method of replenishment

Use the steps identified in this document.

      1.   Define the Problem

---

[33] http://www.fe.doe.gov/index.html

2. Identify alternative solutions

3. Identify future outcomes

4. Identify returns, Positive or Negative

5. Select & implement modeling technique

6. Decide

7. Review the results

Using the class as a population, construct and perform a Delphi to solve the problem(s) that you have identified.

Putting it all together, developing the appropriate environment

> "Punishing honest mistakes stifles creativity. I want people moving and shaking the earth, and they're going to make mistakes."
>
> —H. Ross Perot, Founder, EDS

So far we've been concentrating on the tools, both qualitative and quantitative. If the corporate environment does not foster clear exchange of information, decisions will not be made. In Up the Organization, Townsend says that you've got to play "You Bet Your Job" occasionally. How do you establish an organization that allows people to make decisions, knowing that some of them will be wrong?

Making the final Decision

Once upon a time, back in the European Middle Ages, the small city-states were involved in constant wars. The Gosdorks[34] were especially adept at strategy and tactics. In a war with a small Blogrod army, the Gosdorks had the Blogrod positioned so that they were attacking uphill on a hot day with the sun directly in their eyes. Normally, in this situation, the Blogrod general would surrender honorably and they all would go home for cocktails, having saved their honor. However, this Blogrod general decided to fight, and fight they did. Blogrodistan won the day, as the Gosdorks had never been up against such an uncivilized general, one that refused to follow the civilized rules. I may have the story wrong, or it just might be a nice fairy tale, however the message is quite clear.

---

[34] I don't remember the names of the actual combatants, so I made these up.

You did not get into the position where you have to make this decision by accident. You have worked your way up through the ranks and are now expected to do your job, and you job is to make decisions. While writing this book, I frequently turned to the Internet for references. I brought up Google and keyed in the words Information Overload. Google returned 5,060,000 references. If I spend 30 seconds looking at each reference – that's 42,166.7 hours; or almost five years, working 24 hours a day, 7 days a week to check each reference. That is a useless statistic; however it does prove a point. There is a common phrase in the Information Technology field: "The Paralysis of Analysis." An excessive amount of information frequently strikes the analyst and leaves him unable to make a decision. This is the primary danger of quantitative information. The analyst feels that, "we need just one more study, just one more set of data." If enough analysis is done, then we hope the problem will disappear of its own volition. Unfortunately...

For example, over the last three years there has been a 300 percent increase in the rate of leprosy in the USA. That is an impressive statistic. However, when you examine the number – we come up with the probability of getting Leprosy has climbed to .23%. That is 23 cases in a population of 10,000 people of a disease that is easily treated with antibiotics[35]. The disease is commonly spread by exposure to armadillos. One source that I found refers to the, "shocking rise in incidence of Leprosy." Does that sound like we have an infestation of armadillos in this country?

In his classic management book, Up the Organization, Robert Townsend defines and discusses the word decision:

---

[35] http://100777.com/node/501

"All decisions should be made as low as possible in the organization. The Charge of the Light Brigade was ordered by an officer who wasn't there looking at the territory. There are two types of decisions: those that are expensive to change and those that are not. A decision to build the Edsel or Mustang (or locate your factory in Orlando or Yakima) should not be made hastily; nor without plenty of inputs from operating people or specialists. But the common garden-variety decision – like when to have the cafeteria open for lunch or what brand of pencils to buy – should be made fast. No point in taking three weeks to make a decision that can be made in three seconds – and corrected inexpensively later if wrong. The whole organization may be out of business while you oscillate between baby blue and buffalo-brown coffee cups"

Another point of view about decision-making can be gathered from the fascinating book on leadership "Leadership Secrets of Attila the Hun.[36]"

(NO, I'm not kidding!) Dr. Roberts lists the "Attilaisms" for Decision Making:

- Every decision involves some risk.
- Time does not always improve a situation for a king or his Huns
- Fundamental errors are inescapable when the unqualified are allowed to exercise judgment and make decisions.
- Quick decisions are not always the best decisions. On the other hand, unhurried decisions are not always the best decisions.
- Chieftains should never rush into confrontation.
- A chieftain's confidence in his decision making preempts name-dropping to his Huns

---

[36]Roberts, Wess, PhD.

- It is unfortunate when final decisions are made by chieftains headquartered miles away from the front, where they can only guess at conditions and potentialities known only to the captain on the battlefield

- When victory will not be sweet, the chieftain keeps his Huns from war.

- The ability to make difficult decisions separates chieftains from Huns.

I don't think I can say much more.

Bibliography

- Anderson, Sweeney and Williams, *Statistics for Business and Economics*, 8th Edition, Mason Ohio
- Dalkey, Norman C. *The Delphi Method: an Experimental Study of Group Opinion*, The Rand Corporation, Santa Monica CA, 1969
- Flomberg, Howard, *Management Decision Theory, Managing Pragmatically, 2nd Ed.* University Readers, San Diego Ca, 2005
- Flomberg, Howard, *Incentive!*, Create Space, 2010
- Gladwell, Malcolm, *blink*, Little and Brown Company, New York, 2005
- Groebner, Shannon, Fry and Smith, *Business Statistics 6th Edition*[37], Pearson Publications, New Jersey, 2005
- Miles, Matthew and Huberman, *Qualitative Data Analysis*, Sage Publications, Newbery Park, CA, 1984

---

[37] The author was a contributor to this textbook. hf

The Author:

Howard Flomberg

Author, Adjunct Professor & Systems Analyst

Howard "Howie" Flomberg teaches people how to make effective business decisions and optimize everyday processes so that they become more productive. His work is based on 30 years as a consultant, college professor and IT systems analyst for Fortune 500 companies.

Howie's passion for technology is matched by his desire to share knowledge with business leaders, innovators and students. He began teaching at his alma mater, Metropolitan State College of Denver, while working in the IT industry. He taught over 1,500 students over 10 years. Valued for his teaching abilities, students praised Howie for his accessibility and humor that "made statistics bearable."

His courses included Decision Theory, presenting both Qualitative and Quantative approaches (defining the pros and cons of potential decisions), Project Management, Systems Analysis and Design, Computer Information Systems.

Howie directly participated in technology advancements, from being an Air Force Maintenance Tech, on a computer that had over 58,000 vacuum tubes and the computing power of a cell phone to garnering a national reputation for exceptional system development and database design. He worked for Ross Perot in two companies and pioneered quality assurance and development methodologies.

Howie's early IT roles included mainframe computer developer, database administrator (DBA) and programmer in industry; and computer technician with the United States Air Force. He earned a B.S. in Management Science and M.S. in Computer Science/ Information Systems after being honorably discharged from the Air Force.

Driven by innovation and service, Howie's most recent book, *Incentive!*, is available on Amazon and other major online booksellers. He is available for teaching, consulting, speaking and writing engagements. He can be reached via Email at *hflomberg@gmail.com*